The Dirty Thirties!

The United States
from 1929–1941

by Mary C. Turck

Perfection Learning®

Book Design: Lisa Lorimor
Cover Design: Michelle Glass

Dedication

To Howard and Millie Turck and Ruth Balto, who shared their depression stories with me, and to Molly Salzberger for helping to edit this book.

About the Author

Mary Turck is a freelance writer who lives in Minnesota with her husband, Ron Salzberger, and their two daughters, Molly and Macy. In addition to being a writer, Mary has also worked as a teacher and a lawyer.

Photo and Art Credits:
© Bettmann/CORBIS: 15, 16, 28, 40, 61; © Museum of History and Industry/CORBIS: 23; © Schenectady Museum; Hall of Electrical History Foundation/CORBIS: 8; Detroit News Archive: 22

ArtToday: 4, 5, 6, 9 (bottom), 10, 12, 27, 38, 42, 55, 62; Corel Studio: 1; Digital Stock: 63; Library of Congress: Cover, 3, 7, 9 (top), 11, 14, 19, 20, 21, 24, 26, 29, 30, 33, 34, 36, 39, 44, 45, 46, 48, 52, 53; National Archives: 57

Table of Contents

CHAPTER 1

Roaring Through the Twenties

At New York's Three Hundred Club, the night roared on. A crowd danced to live jazz. Velvet curtains covered the walls. A glass of water cost $3. **Bootleg** champagne cost $35 a bottle.

Bootleg means "illegal liquor." The Eighteenth **Amendment** to the Constitution became law in 1919. It banned, or prohibited, the sale of alcohol in the United States. People called this law **prohibition**.

Alcohol was illegal. The Three Hundred Club was illegal. But the drinkers and dancers didn't care. They just wanted a good time. The party might last until dawn—unless the police came.

On Wall Street

Later in the morning, Wall Street awakened. It buzzed with excitement. Here people bought and sold **stocks**. Surely this was the center of the country, the center of the whole world!

Wall Street is a short, narrow street in New York City. It forms a triangle with Broad and New Streets. This is where the New York Stock Exchange and many big businesses and banks are located. Wall Street, as the entire financial district is called, is the heart of U.S. banking and business. It is an international symbol of finance.

Wall Street was all about money. Owning stocks meant owning a part of a company.

How Wall Street Works

Mr. X wants to make cars. He needs $100,000 to build the factory and buy materials. He doesn't have the money. So he forms a corporation. The people who buy **shares** will own the corporation.

One thousand people buy shares of Mr. X's corporation. Each person pays $100 per share. That means that each person owns 1/1000 of the corporation for each share bought.

The X Corporation builds the factory and makes cars. It sells lots of cars. At the end of five years, the corporation has made a profit of $200,000. X Corporation invests $100,000 of this profit in a second factory. The remaining $100,000 profit is given back to the shareholders. Each shareholder receives $100, or 1/1000 of the profits, for each

share owned. That payment is called a *dividend*. The shareholders still own their shares. Dividends are paid out of profits. A dividend is one way that people make money on shares of stock.

Now lots of people want to own a piece of X Corporation. They offer to buy the shares from the original investors. Mrs. D decides to sell one share. She paid $100 when she bought the share. Now a new buyer is willing to pay her $300 for that one share. Selling shares is another way that shareholders make money.

What will happen if X Corporation loses money? What if no one wants to buy the cars? Then the stockholders receive no dividends. No one will want to buy their shares.

On Wall Street, investors bought and sold stocks. Men in suits gambled on California oil stocks. Bankers invested in Florida land **schemes**. Stocks doubled and tripled in value. Investors became millionaires.

Money bought fashion. Young men purchased raccoon coats. Young women wore short skirts. Everybody bought cars. The rich paid in cash. The rest bought on **credit**. They paid one dollar down and a dollar a week. The economy grew. The country prospered.

Off Wall Street

Workers hurried to wash and grab a bite of breakfast. Late to work meant losing a job. Factory hours ran from sunup to sundown.

More than 200,000 African Americans lived a few miles from Wall Street. During World War I, black workers came from the South. They came north to escape **racism**. They came north to find jobs. Many found apartments in Harlem.

Harlem is a section of New York City where many African Americans settled during the late 1880s and early 1900s. During the early 1900s, Harlem became the center of African American culture and business.

But African Americans found they could not escape racism. Many parts of New York City kept out black people. Many landlords would not rent to them. Harlem landlords raised rents.

Now two families lived in a space meant for one. Sometimes rooms rented by the work shift. A day worker slept in the room at night. He or she left for work in the morning. Then a night worker used the room during the day. These crowded apartment buildings were called *tenements*.

Each tenement building had many small apartments. Those who lived on upper floors walked up. There were no elevators. People from several apartments shared a single bathroom.

Irish, Polish, Russian, and German **immigrants** filled other tenements. Like the black immigrants from the South, they came to find work. Now they all competed for the same jobs.

More and more immigrants came to Harlem. When they made enough money, many moved out. But **segregation** kept African Americans in Harlem.

In Chicago, the story was the same. It was similar in Detroit. Immigrants filled the nation's cities. They worked hard. The average wage was low. There were more workers than jobs. People did the best they could.

Evelyn worked in a laundry. She was a press operator. She said her job was better than some. The "girls" in the starching department had it worse. They had to stick their hands into "almost boiling starch." The starchers sang **spirituals** as they worked. The singing helped them stand the work.

Evelyn talked to a writer who was part of the Federal Writers' Project. Evelyn told about her work.

> *Cold starch is better, but hot starch is cheaper— and you know the bosses. . . . The starchers used to sing, "Go Down Moses," "Down By The Riverside," and . . . the feeling they put in their singing . . . lifted up our spirits and we joined in sometimes. That was too much pleasure to have while working for his money said the boss, and the singing was cut out.*

The Federal Writers' Project started during the **depression**. The government paid writers to interview and write about ordinary people across the country. These writers wrote stories of life and work. Many of these stories are in the American Memories collection, part of the Library of Congress.

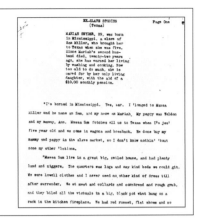

People worked hard. The economy grew. The country prospered. But one worker in ten was unemployed. Six families out of ten lived in poverty. The top five percent of the population received one-third of all the income.

On the Farm

In Minnesota, Henry and Mary headed for the barn. He carried the lantern, and she carried the baby. Milking time came early every morning. The baby hung in a homemade swing. He watched the gentle cows eat. His mother and father milked them by hand. The kerosene lantern cast a warm circle of light. Electricity had not yet come to their farm.

Typical Midwest farm family

Farm prices plunged after World War I. Some farmers lost their farms. Those who stayed often struggled to pay their **mortgages**.

A mortgage is a kind of loan. Henry's father borrowed money from a bank. He promised to pay back some money each November. He pledged their farm for the loan. That meant if the payments weren't made, the bank would take the farm.

In the South, millions of black farmers had no land. Some farmed as **tenants**. A tenant rented a farm, paying rent to the landowner each year.

African American farmer

Other black farmers were **sharecroppers**. They didn't own the land and didn't pay cash rent. Instead, they paid a percentage of the crops. A family might pay one-third of their cotton as rent.

Tenants and sharecroppers often borrowed money. Usually, they borrowed from the landlord. No one else would lend to them. They borrowed to buy seeds or food. These farmers paid back the loans at harvesttime. If the harvest was good, they might have money left over. If the harvest was bad, they would owe more than they had.

Tenant farmers and sharecroppers led hard lives. They did not even own their homes. Their landlords acted as if they owned the workers as well as the land.

In the West, **migrant** farmworkers harvested crops. These workers moved from place to place. One week they picked lettuce. The next week they moved on. At the next farm, they picked strawberries. Later in the summer, they picked tomatoes.

Many migrant workers came from Mexico. They lived at the mercy of crops, weather, and employers. They earned little. They lived in shacks or tents. And they spent their lives on the road.

Farmers everywhere felt left out. Once farming meant eating well. Now farming meant going broke. Once farmers were models for the country. Now they were hayseeds or hicks.

Rural communities suffered along with farmers. When farmers had no money, they could not buy clothes. They could not buy cars. They could not repay their loans. The clothing store had less money. The car dealer had less money. And so did the banker. In 1928, some 549 rural banks failed.

CHAPTER 2

All fall Down

In 1929, investors "played" the **market**. They took chances. They borrowed money from the bank to buy stocks. Or they bought stocks on margin. They spent money they did not have. When stock prices went up, they sold at huge profits.

Everyone talked about the market. *The New York Times* printed stock-price lists. It also printed a stock index. This index showed the rise and fall of each stock price. The market was exciting. It was the biggest game in town.

Playing the Market

Let's say Mr. Y decides to play the stock market. He borrows $3,000 from the bank. He buys 10 shares of Pacifica Oil on January 1. Each share costs him $100. Every day Mr. Y looks at stock prices in the newspaper.

At the end of March, Pacifica shares are selling for $200 each! Mr. Y has doubled the value of his stocks. He feels great!

Now Mr. Y decides to buy more shares. He still has $2,000 in the bank. He buys ten more shares. Now he has 20 shares total. At the end of June, Pacifica shares are selling for $400. Mr. Y's shares are now worth $8,000!

If Mr. Y were to sell the shares now, he could pay back the bank. He would have a profit of about $5,000. ($8,000 minus his investment of $3,000 plus **interest** charged by the bank.)

But Mr. Y doesn't want to sell. He wants more stock. And so does everyone else.

Buying on Margin

Mr. Z buys 100 shares of TNT stock. The price of the shares is $5,000. Mr. Z doesn't have $5,000. He is sure that he will make money on the stock. So he pays his **broker** $500. The broker loans him the other $4,500. The broker, in turn, borrows the $4,500 from a bank.

At any time, the broker can **call in** the loan. This is a margin call. If the stock is still worth $5,000, Mr. Z can sell it. Then he can pay the broker. He will break even. If the stock is worth $6,000, Mr. Z will make a profit of $1,000 less the broker's fee.

As long as stock prices rise, Mr. Z will make money, and the broker will collect a percentage of the profit for his fee. Then the broker will pay back the bank plus interest.

But if the stock is worth less than $5,000, Mr. Z will lose money. He will not have money to pay the broker. The broker will lose money, and he will not be able to pay the bank. The bank will lose money.

To some people, the stock market seemed like a great way to make money. Others were not so sure. What went up, they feared, would come down. The stock market seemed like gambling.

Panic on Wall Street, October 29, 1929

Stock Market Crash

Warning signs appeared early. The market shook. Stock prices dropped, recovered, and fell again. Then came the crash.

October 24, 1929, was Black Thursday. People panicked. They tried to sell their stocks. Prices fell sharply.

The end came on October 29. This was Black Tuesday. More stocks were sold than ever before. Prices fell more than they ever had. And they kept falling.

People who bought stocks on margin lost. They could not pay the margin calls. Their brokers lost. They could not repay the banks. The bankers lost. Their banks **failed** and closed.

One Wall Street investor described the situation to writer Studs Terkel years later.

> *Everybody was stunned. Nobody knew what it was all about. [Wall] Street had general confusion. They didn't understand it any more than anybody else. They thought something would be announced.*

For two weeks, the market sank. By mid-November, $40 billion was gone. In September, *The New York Times* stock average had been 542. That was the average number of shares traded. Now it was only 224.

Slowly, the news sank in. Rich people realized they were now broke. Investors understood they had lost everything.

Many people gave up. Some wandered the streets in a daze. Some even killed themselves. The suicide rate rose to an all-time high.

Louis "Studs" Terkel was born in Chicago, Illinois, in 1912. For most of his life, he has been best known as "the person asking the questions."

For over 40 years, Terkel worked as an interviewer on his daily, one-hour show broadcast from WFMT in Chicago. His radio show, which included many interviews, began in 1954 and ended in 1988.

Terkel is as well known for his books as he is for his radio shows. His most admired books are oral histories. For *Hard Times: An Oral History of the Great Depression*, Terkel collected stories of how people survived one of the toughest periods in American history.

Banking Collapse

Banks started failing early. Throughout the 1920s, banks failed. Each year saw an average of 635 failures. When a bank failed, **depositors** lost their money.

After the crash, more banks failed. During 1930, bank failures reached 1,352. Many failed because of bad loans. They had loaned money during the 1920s. Now people had no money to repay those loans. Some banks made bad investments. Now they had only worthless stock. Others failed because of runs on the banks.

A Run on the Bank

Banks operate on money and trust. Depositors put their money in the bank. The bank promises to pay interest on the deposit. Interest is like a fee for using the money.

The bank loans out depositors' money. The depositors trust the bankers. They believe that the bankers will make good loans. Bankers believe that the debtors will pay back the loans—with interest.

Banks always have some cash. If a depositor wants money, the bank pays it out. But banks do not have enough cash to pay all the depositors at the same time.

What happens when many depositors demand their money? This is known as *a run on the bank*. The bank cannot pay off all of these depositors at once. So the bank runs out of money, or fails.

Raymond Tarver worked for a bank in Georgia. That bank failed. He got another job. Later, he told his story to a writer from the Federal Writers' Project.

Not only my job was in the balance but my savings were gone, at least for the present.

No one knows, unless they have experienced it, what it means to work in a place under such conditions. Of course, there were promises that the bank would soon open up and resume business and begin paying off. That gave the depositor something to hope for at least. The sad part was, this was the strongest bank in this town. In fact there had already been several failures, so this was almost the only bank open for business. It was a national bank too, so everybody thought his or her money was safe. We worked on a while. To be frank, I didn't worry so much about my losses. I was so concerned about the other fellows. People were losing their homes and some their savings of a lifetime. The saddest part of it was to see widows who probably had been left a little insurance and had put it all in the bank. People have a feeling that all connected with a bank, from the directors, president, on down to the lowest employee, are responsible for a bank failure and that makes you feel bad.

Disappearing Jobs

Most people owned no stocks. Many had no bank accounts. The crash still hit them hard.

Factories laid off workers. Businesses closed. People lost jobs. About three million people lost their jobs in 1930.

Another four million lost their jobs the next year. By 1933, one worker in four was unemployed.

Without a job, a worker had no money. The family could not pay rent. They could not buy food or clothes.

One woman told author Studs Terkel about her family's experience.

> *I remember all of a sudden we had to move. My father lost his job and we moved into a double garage. The landlord didn't charge us rent for seven years. We had a coal stove, and we had to each take turns, the three of us kids, to warm our legs. . . . In the morning, we'd get out and get some snow and put it on the stove and melt it and wash around our faces. Never the neck or anything. Put on our two pairs of socks on each hand and two pairs of socks on our feet and long underwear and lace it up with Goodwill shoes. Off we'd walk, three, four miles to school.*

Her family was lucky. They still had a place to live. Other families were homeless. Some lived under bridges. Some begged for food at the back doors of those who still had homes.

Just Around the Corner

Herbert Hoover was the president during these difficult times. He believed in confidence. He thought that people needed to have confidence in the economy. He hoped that predicting **prosperity** would bring it back.

So he said the depression would not last. In March 1930, he predicted the end would happen in 60 days. A few months later, he announced that the depression was over. Over and over, he insisted better days were just around the corner.

CHAPTER 3

Making Do

Self-Help

Forty unemployed men met in Seattle. They wanted to help themselves and their families. They started the Unemployed Citizens' League (UCL). Soon they had 50,000 members. UCL workers did any work they could find. They cut firewood. They fished. They harvested food from cooperating farms. They shared everything they received.

When a member family was **evicted** from its home, UCL took action. Members went to the home. They moved the people and furniture back into the house. Each time the landlord threw them out, the UCL moved them back in. The law said the landlord could evict people if they didn't pay rent. The UCL didn't care about the law. They protected their members.

Within the UCL, people **bartered**. They traded work for *scrip*, or unofficial money. The UCL printed its own scrip. Members used scrip to pay one another for work.

One man fixed shoes. Another fixed cars. Another cut hair. The man who fixed shoes would be paid in scrip. Then he would pay the scrip to another member for a haircut.

A haircut paid for with scrip

19

The Seattle city government saw what the UCL did. They thought it was a good idea. So the mayor's office worked with the UCL. They set up centers to distribute food and clothing. Needy people worked on city projects. They were paid in food and clothing.

Across the country, people formed self-help groups like the UCL. But self-help was not enough. The self-help groups could share only what they had. They did not have enough resources to feed themselves. As one person observed, "It's like a starving dog eating his own tail."

Selling Apples

Men who could find no other work sold apples or pencils. They set up shoe-shine stands on the corners. They tried to save a little **dignity**. At least they were not quite begging.

A surplus of apples in 1930 started the apple-selling business. A man could buy a box of 72 apples for $1.75. He would sell them for a nickel each. If he sold all the apples, his profit would be $1.85.

Then the apple shippers raised the price of a box to $2.25. That cut the seller's profit to $1.35. Every bad apple in the box cut the profit by another nickel.

President Hoover approved of selling apples. He even said that some people left their jobs "for the more profitable one of selling apples."

Soup Kitchens and Bread Lines

Churches and synagogues responded to the crisis. New York Rabbi Rosenblum preached to his congregation. "Fifty thousand children are in need of feeding," he said. "We cannot keep them alive on prayers. We must give them bread."

Some groups set up soup kitchens. They made soup from old vegetables

and bones. Soup was a cheap food to make. Volunteers tended big soup kettles. They fed bowls of soup to the hungry.

Some groups handed out bread to lines of hungry people. Eating bread every day might get boring. But it kept people alive.

Community organizations joined in. So did city and state governments. Even their best efforts were not enough.

Unemployment bred bitterness. People hated taking **charity**. They wanted to work for a living. But there was no work.

21

Men felt especially bad. They wanted to support their families and feed their children. They believed this was their duty as husbands and fathers. When they could not find work, they felt like failures.

Unemployed men dressed for work each morning. They left their houses with newspapers in hand. Each day, they worked their way through the want ads. Each day, they walked from door to door, looking for jobs. Each day, the story was the same—no work.

After weeks of job hunting, the men's shoes were worn thin. So were the men. Still, they left their houses each morning. They no longer bothered to look for work. They knew there was no work. Instead, they went to the public library. There they could sit in a warm place. They could read a newspaper without paying for it.

They stayed away from home all day. They did not want to be there at lunchtime. They did not want to see the small portions their children were given. They did not want to be tempted to eat some of their scarce food.

Parents grew desperate. They had no food. They had no jobs. Many stole. In some cities, mobs took food from stores.

In Minneapolis, Minnesota, women broke into a grocery store. They made a list of the food they took. They promised to pay for it "someday." They could not let their children starve.

Hoovervilles

As people struggled to feed their families, their bills went unpaid. Buying food came before making mortgage payments.

Soon hundreds of thousands of people lost their homes. Lucky families doubled up in small apartments. Unlucky ones lived on the streets. Homeless people slept under bridges.

In many big cities, new **slums** sprang up. Homeless men and women built homes of cardboard. They shared cooking fires. They had no sewers or water pumps. Their "streets" were mud when it rained and dust when it didn't. People named their new communities Hoovervilles for the president who seemed to do nothing.

Hooverville outside Seattle

March on Washington

Military **veterans** were angry. They had risked their lives for their country. Now their country had turned them out onto the streets.

After World War I, Congress promised **bonuses** to veterans. The bonuses were not paid right away. Payments were to start in 1945 and would average $1,000 per veteran. In 1932, that was a good year's wages.

Veterans wanted the bonuses paid early. After the war, the veterans had found jobs. Now there were no jobs. Now the veterans needed the bonus money to live. Many in Congress agreed. They proposed a new bonus bill.

President Hoover said the country could not afford the bonus payment in 1932. So Congress defeated the bill.

Angry veterans marched on Washington. About 300 set out from Portland, Oregon. They rode in boxcars on freight trains. Others joined along the way. Many more traveled on foot.

Thousands of bonus marchers and families came any way they could. Soon, nearly 20,000 bonus marchers arrived in Washington.

The veterans set up 27 camps around the city. Some occupied vacant government buildings.

At first, President Hoover tried to ignore the veterans. Then he decided to drive them out. President Hoover sent in the army led by General Douglas MacArthur. They used tanks, horses, tear gas, and swords. They drove the bonus marchers out of Washington. Then the soldiers burned their camps.

Depression Wisdom

People **scrimped** and saved in every way they could. They made soup from chickens' feet. Clothes had patches on top of patches.

Many homes had coal furnaces. Children and parents went to the railroad tracks. They picked up bits of coal that fell from trains. They used this coal to heat their homes.

Adults and children wore their shoes until there were holes in the soles. Then they put cardboard in the shoes to make them last longer. Children grew out of their shoes. So parents cut holes in the toes.

Ruth Balto's father died when she was five years old. Then the depression came.

Ms. Balto remembers getting clothing from a neighbor. "Hand-me-downs. We were grateful to get them. Beggars can't be choosers."

Ms. Balto was the youngest child. Her two older sisters quit school. They had to work. Ms. Balto was the only one in the family to graduate from high school.

"My sister Annette was the artist," Ms. Balto recalls. "She was in her early teens. A dress manufacturer hired her. They paid Annette to go to a fancy store on Fifth Avenue. The store windows displayed the latest fashions. Annette had to draw the dresses. That was illegal. When she was caught, they gave her a scare."

Ms. Balto explained that Annette did not go to jail. But she had to stop drawing the dresses. She had to look for other ways to make money.

25

Phyllis Brantl remembers her depression childhood. Her parents sold the icebox, bathtub, telephone, rug, good dishes, tablecloths, "anything that would bring a nickel." They needed money to make payments on their farm. With the farm, they had food. Without it, they would have nothing.

Before the depression, her family burned coal for heat. Then they couldn't afford coal any longer. Since they were on a farm, they raised grain. They saved the straw at harvesttime. Then they twisted straw and burned it. Twisting straw was hard work. Straw did not heat as well as coal. But at least it kept them from freezing.

Every family looked for ways to get by. Older children passed clothes down to younger children. When the clothes wore out, scraps of fabric made quilts. Children carried lunches to school. Families could not buy peanut butter. They could not afford to eat meat. Instead, children ate plain bread sandwiches.

The lessons learned lasted for generations. Mothers passed on the following hard-won depression wisdom.

Use it up or wear it out.
Make it do or do without.

CHAPTER 4

FDR and a NEW DEAL

By 1932, people were sick of President Hoover. They blamed him for the depression. And the depression kept getting worse.

To be fair, he did not cause the depression. That was too much to blame on any one man. On the other hand, he did not do much to help.

Hoover thought the economy would improve on its own. He

Herbert Hoover

called the depression "a passing incident in our national lives." He did not believe government needed to act. He thought charities could feed people. He thought government aid would make people lazy.

Campaign and Election

Franklin D. Roosevelt ran against Herbert Hoover in 1932. Roosevelt promised a "new deal." FDR easily won the election. And the Democrats won a majority in Congress. Now they had to get the country out of the depression.

The First 100 Days

Roosevelt took office on March 4, 1933. He gave his first speech as president. "This nation asks for action, and action now!" he said.

Lights burned all night in the White House. The new president was hard at work. On Monday, March 6, he closed every bank in the country. Then he called Congress into session. On March 9, Congress passed the Emergency Banking Act.

On Sunday, March 12, FDR went on the radio. "I want to talk for a few minutes with the people of the United States about banking," he said. He explained the banking system. He told people that banks would reopen the next day. "I can assure you, my friends," he said, "that it is safer to keep your money in a reopened bank than it is to keep it under the mattress."

Roosevelt knew people had lost faith in the banks. Americans were afraid the banks would close. Then they would lose their money. So many people kept their savings at home—close to them.

The people believed the new president. The next day, they deposited money in the banks. And the banks stayed open.

Next, FDR turned to Congress. He asked for new programs. He asked for money for **relief**. Congress agreed.

FDR continued the radio broadcasts. He talked directly to the people. Millions of people tuned in to listen. FDR's Fireside Chats gave them hope.

The people called the broadcasts *fireside chats*. FDR seemed to be in each home, sitting in the living room. Each listener felt like the president was speaking directly to him or her.

Alphabet Soup

FDR promised the people a new deal. This came in the form of programs to help people. All the New Deal programs seemed to have initials. They were the NLRB, CCC, PWA, WPA, NRA, AAA, REA, and more. They made a whole alphabet soup. Some people said the programs would not work. FDR and his team knew that might be true. But they decided to go ahead anyway. They thought it was better to try and fail than not to try at all. If a program failed, they reasoned, they could end it and try again.

CCC—Civilian Conservation Corps

The CCC started a month after FDR took office. The CCC hired young men, ages 18 to 25. They had to be unemployed and out of school. Each man had to weigh more than 107 pounds. He had to stand between 60 and 78 inches tall.

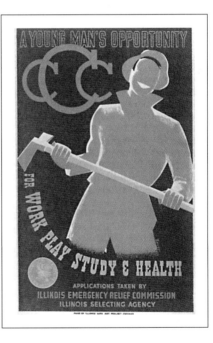

They worked in national forests, on wildlife **refuges**, and on other public land. They built hiking trails and picnic tables. They built roads and outdoor toilets.

These young men planted more than a billion trees. They were called *soil soldiers*. Their work helped preserve the soil and other resources.

The CCC workers left their homes to live in camps. The military housed and fed them. By the end of July, more than 300,000 CCC soldiers were employed. They earned $30 to $45 a month.

More than half said they signed up because they were tired of having nothing to do. Now they worked and went to classes.

"I'm on a great team," one young man wrote home. " . . . we are the army who are training to repel the enemies of the land."

NRA—National Recovery Administration

The NRA worked to control the economy. It asked each industry to draw up a plan. The plan would cover wages, prices, working conditions, and production. Businesses also had to allow **unions**. Workers finally had the right to organize.

NRA plans were **voluntary**. The NRA could not force businesses to cooperate. Instead, it called on their **patriotism**. When a business cooperated, it received a "Blue Eagle." A slogan on the Blue Eagle said, "We do our part."

Some businesses wanted nothing to do with the NRA. They wanted nothing to do with the New Deal and FDR. Henry Ford would not cooperate. He called the Blue Eagle "that Roosevelt buzzard."

Other businesses valued the Blue Eagle. They thought it showed their patriotism. They knew it brought customers. People liked businesses with the Blue Eagle.

Some people thought the NRA codes were bad. They said the codes violated the constitution. The Supreme Court agreed. It struck down the law that set up the NRA. The Blue Eagle died in 1935. But other New Deal programs continued.

FERA—Federal Emergency Relief Administration

FERA gave money to the states for relief. Sometimes relief meant money paid to people. Sometimes it meant free food or clothing. People had to apply for relief. They went to the office and talked to a relief worker.

Louise Armstrong was a social worker. She became a county director for FERA. Later, she wrote a book about her experience. She described her first day on the job.

> *I interviewed over forty applicants that day. There was something strange about these poor people. Nearly all of them, especially the old people, came in apparently terribly frightened. Some of them were trembling so that I could actually see them shake, and at first they could hardly speak.*

She soon found out why. In the past, county relief workers had been mean to people. They looked down on poor people.

FERA tried to change all that. FERA investigators looked at relief programs. Then they reported back to Washington.

Lorena Hickok was one of those investigators. Hickok traveled to Pennsylvania, Kentucky, North Dakota, and New York. She saw people who'd had nothing to eat for days. She heard of babies dying from starvation. She found children whose bare feet were "purple with cold." In one of her reports, she wrote that the people she met with were honest, self-respecting citizens who, through no fault of their own, were temporarily on relief. Most had always managed their own affairs and could be trusted with cash.

CWA to PWA to WPA—Works
Progress Administration

Most people did not want relief. In her book, Louise Armstrong reported one conversation.

> *"Maybe you think I like to come up here beggin'!" the client exclaimed. "I don't want no . . . relief orders! I want work, I tell you! Work! Work! I got to have a job!"*

The FDR administration heard this plea. By the end of 1933, it set up the Civil Works Administration. Millions went to work for the CWA. They built highways, bridges, and tunnels. They built schools, courthouses, libraries, hospitals, and jails.

Eleanor Roosevelt was the president's wife. She worked with him to help poor people. She traveled around the country, serving as FDR's eyes and ears. She insisted that the CWA give work to women as well as men. Women's jobs were limited. Some worked in sewing or nursing programs. Some did secretarial work. But they never earned as much as the men.

All through the winter of 1933–34, people worked for the CWA. Then the program ended.

Other public work programs continued. The Public Works Administration (PWA) began in 1933 and continued to 1939. The Works Progress Administration (WPA) began in 1935.

Some people disliked the public work programs. They thought it was wrong for the government to provide so many jobs. They said WPA workers were lazy.

Some of the WPA workers were writers. Some were artists. The WPA ran an arts program. WPA artists painted 2,566 murals. They produced 17,744 sculptures for public buildings. They wrote and performed plays. They interviewed ordinary people and wrote life stories.

Myron Buxton worked on a WPA job. He told his story to a WPA writer.

*One reason people here don't like WPA is because they don't understand it's not all bums and drunks and **aliens**! Nobody ever explains to them that they'd never have had the new High School . . . if it hadn't been for PWA. They don't stop to figure that new brick sidewalks wouldn't be there, the shade trees wouldn't be all dressed up to look at along High Street and all around town, if it weren't for WPA projects. To most in this town . . . WPA's just a racket, set up to give a bunch of loafers and drunks steady pay to indulge in their **vices**! They don't stop to consider that on WPA are men and women who have traveled places and seen things, been educated and found their jobs folded up and [have] nothing to replace them with.*

Some 2,000 people marched before the White House to demand more WPA projects and jobs.

Many people criticized the arts program. Harry Hopkins ran the WPA. Hopkins talked to an interviewer in 1934. He defended the artists, saying, "They've got to eat just like other people."

NYA—National Youth Administration

For young people, the National Youth Administration (NYA) offered work. Young people on relief could work on NYA jobs. They could work up to 70 hours a month. They could earn a maximum of $25 a month.

Some NYA workers were students. High school students could work three hours a day, seven on Saturdays. For this, they earned up to $6 a month. College students could work up to eight hours a day—for $20 a month.

More Alphabet Soup

The Tennessee Valley Authority (TVA) dammed a river and made electricity. Aid to **Dependent Children** (ADC) was an early welfare program. The Fair Employment Practices Commission (FEPC) investigated racial discrimination. The Federal Housing Administration (FHA) helped people buy homes.

TVA workers

The list of New Deal programs goes on and on. Some programs ended by 1940. Many others still exist.

Other Major New Deal Agencies

AAA—The Agricultural Adjustment Administration advised and assisted farmers and **regulated** farm production.

NLRB—The National Labor Relations Board administered the National Labor Relations Act, which called for fair labor practices.

CCC—The Commodity Credit Corporation supported the Department of Agriculture.

REA—The Rural Electrification Administration aided farmers in the electrification of their homes.

FCA—The Farm Credit Administration provided a credit system for farmers by making long-term and short-term credit available.

SEC—The Securities and Exchange Commission protected the public from investing in unsafe securities and regulated stock market practices.

FCC—The Federal Communications Commission regulated radio, telephone, and telegraph systems.

SSB—The Social Security Board provided a **sound** social security system.

FSA—The Farm Security Administration helped farmers buy needed equipment.

USHA—The United States Housing Authority aided in the development of adequate housing throughout the nation.

HOLC—The Home Owners Loan Corporation granted long-term mortgage loans at low cost to homeowners with financial difficulties.

CHAPTER 5

A Separate America

The African American Experience of the Depression

Clifford Burke remembers the depression. Years later, living in Chicago, he talked to Studs Terkel.

The Negro was born in depression. It didn't mean too much to him. The Great American Depression, as you call it. . . . It only became official when it hit the white man.

A tenant farmer

The depression hit African Americans hard. When times were good, they were the last hired. When times went bad, they were the first fired.

Elmer Thomas worked as a meat packer in Chicago. He was African American. He talked to a writer from the Federal Writers' Project. Thomas described the discrimination he observed.

*You take pork packing. Jobs like that, they're clean, easy, light. You won't find Negroes working there. They won't give them such jobs. When they **raise a gang**, you can bet you won't use any Negroes coming in.*

Like in '33, they were hiring young white boys, 16 and 18 years old, raw kids, didn't know a thing, but there were plenty of colored boys waiting for the same chance who never got it.

Hank Johnson, just the other night said he'd bet there hadn't been a Negro hired in Armour's in 7 years. He knows what he's talking about.

Black people had a hard time getting relief. They had a harder time getting jobs. By 1930, half of all black Americans were unemployed.

Elias Covington lived in Laurinburg, North Carolina. In 1935, he worked for 50 cents a day. His father had died. He took care of his mother and a younger brother and sister. He recalled the times in an article for *American Visions* magazine.

In Laurinburg, nobody was making any money. It was a tough time for all Americans, and especially African Americans who were already poor to begin with due to discrimination and the aftermath of slavery.

Then Covington heard about the CCC. The CCC paid $30 a month. "Plus we got all of our clothes, and a clean bed to sleep in. They also had educational facilities and a medical officer."

When the local CCC supervisor asked if he wanted to join, Covington did not hesitate. "I told him 'Yes.' He moved my age up, that's how I got in. I was 15 years old."

Covington served in a segregated CCC company. He learned to use a typewriter. Then he learned to drive an ambulance. He stayed in the CCC until 1942, when he joined the army. He finished high school, then college. He stayed in the army for 20 years, retiring in 1962.

Working for Changes

Eleanor Roosevelt

Eleanor Roosevelt visited the South. She inspected New Deal programs. She saw racial discrimination, and she fought against it.

Mrs. Roosevelt told the president what she saw. She asked him to fight discrimination. FDR ordered an end to discrimination in government programs. His orders helped. So did the knowledge that Mrs. Roosevelt was watching.

In 1938, the president's wife went to Alabama. She attended a conference there. Alabama law required segregation. Under law, whites had to sit in the white section of the auditorium. Blacks had to sit in the black section. Mrs. Roosevelt refused to sit in the white section. She sat with the blacks.

FDR set up a Division of Negro Affairs in the NYA. He appointed Mary McLeod Bethune to head it. Ms. Bethune was a strong black woman and a civil rights advocate. She was also a friend of Eleanor Roosevelt. She helped form the "Black Cabinet." This was a group of about 40 black men and women in the FDR administration. They advised the administration on racial justice.

The Mexican American Experience of the Depression

Migrant farmworker

During the 1920s, a half million Mexicans came to the United States. That brought the total number of Mexican Americans to about 1.5 million. Most of them lived in the west. Many were migrant farmworkers.

Others moved north to work in factories. Like black workers, Mexicans were given the worst jobs. They also suffered racism.

A Michigan woman talked to a researcher in 1930. "I resent the Mexicans being brought in here," she complained. "My cousins [from Serbia] can't get [into this country] and yet they bring these lower elements in."

In the early years of the depression, the government had stopped most immigration. Many Mexican Americans were citizens of the United States. They were not immigrants. They had been born in this country. But they still faced racism. Some cities would not give relief to Mexican Americans. Some Mexican Americans left.

Researchers talked to Mexican Americans in Gary, Indiana. "This is my country," said one young woman bitterly, "but after the way we have been treated I hope never to see it again."

Farmworkers Organize

In California, Mexican American farmworkers organized a union. They tried to **strike** for better wages. The sheriff arrested and jailed them. Growers cut wages. Workers staged another strike.

The **Communist** Party/USA sent help. Communist organizers worked with the union. They believed in taking the side of workers against bosses.

Many people feared the Communists. They thought Communists would take over the country. Communists became special targets of the police. They were sent to jail for years.

Farmworkers strike in California in 1933

The Cannery and Agricultural Workers Industrial Union represented farmworkers. The union organized 400 Mexican American, Filipino, Japanese, and white workers. They worked in orchards in northern California. The largest orchard owner promised $1.40 for an eight-hour day. Then he cut wages to $1.25 for a nine-hour day.

CAWIU called a strike. During the strike, workers refused to work. They demanded that the bosses treat them better or pay higher wages. The strike was the workers' weapon. When they did not work, the employer lost money.

Ministers preached against the union. Growers brought in strikebreakers. The strikebreakers picked fruit. That meant the orchard owners still made money.

The sheriff deputized 200 civilians. They beat union leaders, then jailed them. Eventually, the strikers had to give up.

In 1933, cotton pickers went on strike. They quickly came under attack. "We protect our farmers here," said a sheriff's deputy in Kern County, California. "But the Mexicans are trash . . . We herd them like pigs."

Strikers fought with strikebreakers, growers, and law officers. Soon three strikers were shot to death. Five children of striking farmworkers died of malnutrition.

FERA sent food to the strikers. The NRA put pressure on growers to settle. Finally they did.

That was the last CAWIU victory. In 1934, the growers crushed the union. Eighteen of its leaders were arrested. They were sent to jail for organizing the workers. The union died.

Then desperate farmers from the dust bowl arrived. They took the jobs of Mexican migrant workers. More than 100,000 migrants were sent back to Mexico.

Dust Bowl is the name given to a region of the southwestern United States. The area receives a small amount of rainfall during the year. Therefore, wheat and grass for grazing animals is grown.

During the early 1930s, less than the normal amount of rain fell in parts of this region. The hardest-hit region included the panhandles of Texas and Oklahoma, southwestern Kansas, and southeastern Colorado. Damage from dust storms spread north into Nebraska, South Dakota, Wyoming, Montana, and North Dakota.

Nothing grew in the area, so the slightest winds would whip the dust and dirt into the air. These frequent winds blew topsoil clear across the continent to the Atlantic Coast and far out into the Gulf of Mexico.

Farmhouses were often hidden behind drifts of dust. People had to wear handkerchiefs or masks to keep the dust out of their mouths, noses, and lungs.

Farming families soon left their lands and headed west. They took jobs where they could find them. Most became migrant workers.

All for One and One for All?

Sometimes unions overcame racism. Workers united in a common cause. They saw that they needed to work together. Dora Jones organized **domestic** workers in New York. Domestic workers included maids and cleaning ladies.

Pat Christie was an Irish packinghouse worker in Chicago. In the packinghouses, workers butchered cows and pigs. They cut up and packed the meat for market. Ms. Christie talked to a writer from the Federal Writers' Project in 1939. She, too, told of the union bringing people together.

> *They usually put the colored girls on that vinegar job. Me and another girl used to do a lot of talking and they knew we were in the CIO union so they stuck us on that job to get on our nerves and maybe make us quit. Well, it worked, but not until all the girls had union cards, so much good that one was. All the colored girls, they jump at the chance to be in the union as soon as they're asked. . . .*
>
> *The Polish girls, some of them they'll say, "Let my husband join. Let my husband go to meetings. Let the men do it, it's not for women to do." But once they get interested, boy, oh boy, they'll get up and talk their hearts out and they'll fight like troopers for the union. Once they really get the idea and the feel of the union, you can't hold them down. . . .*
>
> *And the Mexican women, they're all fighters. They know their rights and they fight for all they can get, every time. A boss can't say boo to them, they'll come right back at him.*

CHAPTER 6

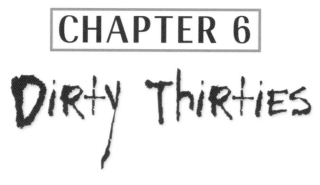

On the Prairie

During the 1920s, farmers moved into the southern plains. They brought tractors to plow the prairie. A man with a team of horses could plow only 3 acres a day. With a tractor, he could plow 50 acres.

Soon the prairie turned to fields. Green grass gave way to golden wheat. Lawrence Svobida farmed in Kansas. More than half a century after the depression, he talked to a PBS (Public Broadcasting Service) reporter. "It was breathtaking," he remembers, "hundreds of acres of wheat that were mine. To me it was the most beautiful scene in all the world."

Then the rain stopped. Without rain, the wheat would not grow. In 1931, the land dried up. For eight years, the rain stayed away.

An Oklahoma family seeks shelter during a dust storm.

March 1936: A dust storm rises over the Texas Panhandle.

Black Blizzards

As the land dried up, the winds came. Once grass had held the soil in place. Now the winds found plowed fields. They swept loose soil into the air. Dark clouds covered the land.

Melt White remembers the time during a PBS interview.

It kept getting worse and worse. And the wind kept blowing harder and harder. It kept getting darker and darker. And the old house is just a-vibratin' like it was gonna blow away. And I started trying to see my hand. And I kept bringing my hand up closer and closer and closer and closer. And I finally touched the end of my nose and I still couldn't see my hand. That's how black it was.

Dust sifted into homes through closed windows. Dust choked people and animals. Children and adults died from dust pneumonia.

This highway in Oklahoma was covered by drifting soil.

Dust Bowl

By 1934, about 35 million acres of land were stripped. The rich soil needed to nourish plants is called *topsoil*. It blew away. Once the fields had produced wheat. Now they grew nothing

The plains had seen wind and drought before. But at that time, the plains had been covered with grass. Now they were plowed. The soil lay open to the wind. The combination of poor farming methods and drought had turned the land to a dust bowl.

In 1935, Congress declared soil **erosion** "a national menace." The Soil Conservation Service went to work. The SCS paid farmers to try new methods.

The new methods could help to hold soil in place. But nothing would help until the rains returned.

Drought Beyond the Dust Bowl

The drought spread beyond the dust bowl. By 1934, it affected 75 percent of the country. Corn once grew head-high. During the drought, it barely made 16 inches. Wheat grew just a few inches tall.

Dust storms blew over the whole country. Dust came in through closed windows. Dust darkened the skies. "But we didn't even have it so bad as other places," one Minnesota dairy farmer remembers. "Most of our land was pasture and hay. That held the soil. Other places, it all blew away."

Okies and Arkies

One person in four left the dust bowl during the thirties. "The land just blew," a Kansas preacher said. "We had to go somewhere." Two and a half million people moved out.

Many went to California. California was the golden state—the promised land. California was the land of hope. There, tired farmers thought, they could grow crops again.

They were mistaken. California had no room for penniless farmers. California's fertile land belonged to large farmers. The only work was stoop labor. Stoop labor meant working bent over. Bending over with a hoe, workers chopped weeds from cotton. Bent over with sacks on their backs, they picked cotton. Stooped, workers picked tomatoes and lettuce.

In the San Joaquin Valley, a stoop laborer could earn $1 a day. A tar paper shack cost 25 cents a day. The shacks had no floors or bathrooms.

Food came from a company-owned store. Prices were always higher there. But by the end of a long work day, the stoop workers had no other choices.

Men, women, and children worked. They were paid by the amount of cotton chopped or fruit picked. Even a child could add a little to the family income.

The migrants from the east were called Okies or Arkies. They faced discrimination and contempt. The people in California did not welcome them.

Down and Out in California

The New Deal tried to help the migrants. The Farm Security Administration built 13 camps. Some camps had tents on wooden floors. Others had metal shelters.

The Arvin Migratory Labor Camp was built at Weedpatch, California. The camp had 106 metal shelters. It also had 98 tents and 20 adobe houses. About 650 people lived there year-round. During cotton-picking season, the camp housed 1,200 people.

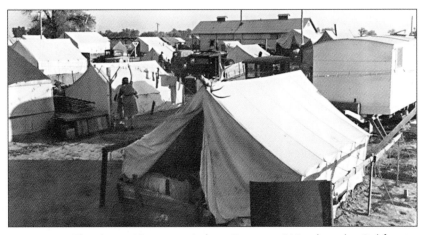

The Arvin Migratory Labor Camp at Weedpatch, California

People living in the adobe homes paid $8.25 per month. They could live there permanently. People in tents and shelters paid 25 cents a week. They had to leave after a year. Many left and returned, unable to find other homes.

Fighting for the Farm

Farmers outside the dust bowl could still raise crops. The threat to their farms came from debt.

When farmers borrowed money, they signed mortgages. They used their property as **security** for loans. If a farmer repaid the loan, the mortgage was done.

48

But sometimes a farmer couldn't make the payments, so he was **in default**. The bank took the farmer's property and sold it to pay off the loan. This process is known as *foreclosure*.

Low prices kept farmers broke. They borrowed money to keep going. When farmers borrowed, they had to mortgage their land. Often, they also mortgaged crops and livestock. If they needed a loan, they had no choice. Just one more year, they thought. If we can make a crop, the prices may get better. If the prices get better, we can pay back these loans. We can make money again.

On the farm, the depression began early. Grain prices dropped in the 1920s. By 1933, all farm prices were down. Hog prices fell below three cents a pound. One farmer shipped some pigs to market. He owed more for the shipping cost than he was paid for the pigs. Oscar Heline farmed in Iowa. He burned grain for fuel. It was cheaper than coal.

Each year, prices dropped more. Farmers could not pay their loans. Bankers foreclosed. Then the farmers rebelled.

Penny Auction to Farm Holiday

Penny auctions began in Nebraska. Theresa Von Baum and her husband owned 80 acres there. After her husband died, Theresa kept farming. She had a mortgage of $442. She could not make the payments.

The local banker knew Theresa. He knew how hard she and her sons worked. He waited for payments. Then in 1932, the local bank failed. A **receiver** took over the mortgage. The new owner of the Von Baum mortgage did not know the family. Nor did he care. A foreclosure sale was set for October 6, 1932.

Theresa Von Baum was not the first farmer to face foreclosure. But she was the first to see a penny auction.

On the day of the sale, thousands of people came to her farm. Farmers talked to the man in charge of the auction. They told him they would pay $100 for the mortgage. He refused.

The sale proceeded. A huge crowd of farmers watched. Someone bid 5 cents for a cow. No one bid more. Six horses were sold for less than $6 total. Machinery was sold for 25 cents. This way, everything sold for very little money.

At the end of the sale, the farmers took up a collection. They paid the man in charge of the sale all the money that had been bid. It was just over a hundred dollars. He gave back the mortgage. Then the farmers gave the animals and equipment back to Theresa Von Baum.

Penny auctions continued. So did other forms of rebellion. Sometimes farmers became violent. One judge was tarred and feathered. Another was threatened with hanging.

In 1932, farmers organized a national farm holiday. Their slogan was "Stay at Home—Buy Nothing—Sell Nothing."

The farm holiday started at the end of August. In some places, farmers blocked highways. Nail-studded planks barred the way for trucks carrying livestock.

In 1933, several states passed mortgage **moratorium** laws. These laws suspended foreclosures. They said no farms could be taken from farmers. The laws helped some farmers. They did not help those who were already in default. They did not apply to mortgages on livestock and machinery. Protests continued.

Gradually, the depression wore down farmers. They no longer believed protest would do any good. They no longer had any energy left. As the New Deal began, farmers turned to it for help.

AAA—Agricultural Administration Act

Farm prices and farm mortgages crippled farmers. The AAA attacked both problems.

First, the AAA asked farmers to limit production. With fewer hogs going to market, prices would rise. That was the idea.

The AAA bought more than six million pigs. They paid 6 to 9 cents per pound. The pigs were slaughtered.

People were outraged. Attorney Clarence Darrow called it a crime to "kill little pigs and throw them out on the prairies to decay while millions are hungry." Many others agreed.

Soon the AAA changed this program. It still bought pigs. Now it slaughtered them and gave the meat to relief programs.

In the west, ranchers raised cattle, not pigs. Drought parched the western states. When grass didn't grow, cows didn't eat. Herds of cattle grew thin and bony.

Farmers watched helplessly. They had no money. There was no hay to buy anyway. The government bought their hungry cows.

The government paid $14 to $20 per cow. Cows that were fit to eat were butchered. The meat went to relief programs.

In the beginning, more than half the cows were unfit to eat. They were too thin, too sick, or too near death. Those cows were simply killed and buried.

Next came shelter belts. Shelter belts were rows of trees. The trees slowed or stopped wind. They help hold soil in place. The New Deal planted trees from Canada to Texas.

Another AAA program was ever-full granaries. The AAA loaned money to farmers to store wheat and corn. The grain would be a food reserve in time of need. When prices rose, the farmers would sell the grain. Then they could pay back the AAA loan.

More Help for Farmers

The Farm Credit Administration loaned money to farmers. This program paid off old mortgages. Then it gave farmers new mortgages at better rates.

Some farmers also found work with the PWA or WPA. Henry Turck and his team of horses plowed roads in winter. They hauled gravel for roads in summer. The WPA salary helped keep the farm family going.

Most farms had no electricity. In 1935, Congress established the Rural Electrification Administration. The REA organized cooperatives. In a cooperative, people join together to buy or sell something. Farmers cooperated by pooling their money. Together, they were able to buy electricity at a lower price. The cooperatives brought electricity to rural areas.

Henry Turck's son, Howard, remembers when electricity came to their farm. "The cows just went nuts," he said. "They were jumping up and down. They tried to get out of the barn. They didn't milk very good for a couple of days." Electric lights made pre-dawn milking easier for farmers. And, eventually, the cows adjusted.

REA worker

CHAPTER 7

America Divided

Who Speaks for America?

Franklin Roosevelt won the presidency by seven million votes in 1932. Even more people voted for him in 1936. He won by ten million votes. He won again in 1940 and 1944. FDR was the nation's longest-serving president.

In his second inaugural address, FDR set forth a vision. "I see one-third of the nation ill-housed, ill-clad, ill-nourished," he said. This was not good enough. Instead, he insisted, "... the test of our progress is not whether we add more to the abundance of those who have much; it is whether we provide enough for those who have too little."

Clearly, FDR spoke for many Americans. But some disagreed.

FDR's inauguration, 1941

Against FDR

Most businessmen did not like FDR. They thought he had too much power. They did not like government power.

Others called FDR crazy. They spread rumors about him. Polio had made him crazy. He was addicted to drugs. The rumors did not last. People could look at FDR and see that the rumors were false.

Some people hated FDR. Usually, they hated Eleanor even more. They hated her plain speaking. They hated her political involvement. They hated her civil rights stands.

The Radio Priest

Father Charles Coughlin tried to speak for America. He began as a pastor of a small church in Royal Oak, Michigan. The Ku Klux Klan was active there. The Klan hated Catholics. It burned a cross at Father Coughlin's church. All this happened in the 1920s.

Father Coughlin went on the radio. He spoke about social justice. He spoke against Communists. He also spoke against the wealthy.

Then came the depression. The radio priest spoke against bankers. He called President Hoover "the Holy Ghost of the rich." His audience grew. Millions of people listened to the radio priest. Listeners sent him 80,000 letters weekly.

At first, the radio priest liked FDR. He said the country could choose "Roosevelt or ruin."

Later, he turned against FDR. In one of his broadcasts, he said FDR had "a government of the bankers, by the bankers, and for the bankers." He also said Communists had taken over the New Deal.

Communists and bankers together? That sounds strange. The radio priest soon became even stranger. He talked against Jews. By 1940, he praised Hitler.

Adolf Hitler was the leader of the German Nazis. They believed that Germans were superior to all other people on Earth, especially Jews.

Hitler became **dictator** of Germany in 1933. He turned Germany into a powerful war machine and started World War II in 1939 by invading Poland. He conquered most of Europe before he was defeated in 1945.

The Townsend Plan

Dr. Frances Townsend thought he spoke for America. He proposed a "cure for depression." He wanted to give $200 a month to senior citizens. Every person over 60 would be paid, as long as they had not been convicted of a crime. They also had to give up all other income. And they had to spend the money every month. That, said Townsend, would get the economy moving.

Many Americans favored Townsend's plan. They wanted old people to have more money. For a brief time, Townsend was very popular.

But where would the money come from? That was the problem. Townsend proposed something like a sales tax. But that would not raise enough money.

In 1935, the New Deal passed the Social Security Act. Social security gave **pensions** to old people.

Social security also helped people who were blind or disabled. It set up a program to help dependent children. The law also set up unemployment insurance. Social security was paid for by payroll taxes. Payroll taxes took a percentage from the paycheck of every worker.

The Social Security Act had some problems. It left out farmers. It left out domestic workers. But it protected many people.

Senator Huey Long— Share Our Wealth

Senator Huey Long came from Louisiana. His father was a **radical**, who was in favor of big political changes. In 1935, he said the country needed a revolution. "What do these rich folks care for the poor man?" asked the older Long. "They care nothing—not for his pain, his sickness, nor his death."

Huey Long agreed with his father. He believed that rich people had too much money and power. Two percent of the people owned 60 to 70 percent of the wealth. That was not fair, said Huey Long. The money needed to be redistributed. Rich people should have less money. Poor people should have more.

First, Huey Long became governor of Louisiana. He was popular. He cared about poor people. He built roads, bridges, and schools.

But Governor Long had a darker side. He was personally **corrupt**. As governor, he was supposed to work for the people. But he worked for himself first. He took money for doing political favors for people. He used politics to make himself rich.

He also acted like a dictator. He used political power to make others do what he wanted. He ordered state legislators to pass his legislation. Some of the laws he wanted were good for people. Some just made Long and his friends rich.

Then Huey Long became a U.S. Senator. As a senator, Long was disappointed in FDR. He thought the New Deal was too **conservative**. The New Deal did not take money from the rich. In 1933, Long started a newspaper. Long referred to the rich as "pigs swilling in the trough of luxury."

Huey Long in 1935

Senator Huey Long had a plan. He called it the Share Our Wealth Plan. He started Share Our Wealth clubs. He wanted to limit big fortunes. His plan would put high income taxes on high incomes. It would also increase **inheritance** taxes. Like Dr. Townsend, Long had a grand idea. Like Townsend, he used inaccurate numbers to support his plan.

Huey Long decided to run for president. Then in 1935, Long was **assassinated**. He was shot by a young man. The young man disagreed with Long's political actions. He also was angry at Long because of a personal dispute. Long's Share Our Wealth plan died with him.

Communists and Anti-Communists

The Communist Party/USA was at its strongest in the 1930s. Communists said everyone should share the wealth. They said no one should be rich. No one should own large companies. The government should own big business. Then all the money should go to the people.

But there was a problem. Communists had won a revolution in Russia. Now they ruled Russia. They ruled as dictators and killed their enemies.

Were all Communists the same? Did U.S. Communists plan to

be dictators too? Many people thought so. They were afraid of Communism. They said Communists were enemies of the United States.

Some people said the New Deal was Communist. They thought Communists were powerful and influenced FDR.

The Communist Party/USA never grew very strong. Enemies attacked the party from the outside. Political differences split the party on the inside.

Many other parties had more support. The **Progressive** Party also wanted to take power away from big corporations. It wanted to give more power to the people. Progressive candidates won elections to Congress. A Progressive was governor of Wisconsin. The Minnesota Farmer-Labor Party elected a governor and other public officials. The **Socialist** Party wanted the government to control business. The Socialist Party ran strong candidates for president. All of these parties were much stronger than the Communist Party/USA.

Labor Unions

Labor unions spoke for more and more Americans. During the New Deal, laws were passed to protect unions. For the first time, the government supported unions.

Employers still opposed unions. They said unions were Communist. They fired workers who joined unions. They did worse to union organizers. Some organizers were beaten. Some were even killed.

One Union Story

A New York laundry worker told her union story to a writer from the Federal Writers' Project.

"One day a fellow applied for a job at our place as a sorter and got it," she said. "We didn't think he would be there long because he certainly did not speed up like the rest of us. The boss saw him and asked him if he was sick. He said no. The boss told him he would have to work faster. He laughed at the boss and told him that a man was a damn fool to rush during the first hour when he had seventeen more staring him in the face. I guess the boss felt like firing him but he was a giant of a man and as strong as an ox. The boss let him slide."

At lunchtime, the boss yelled "on the fly." That meant the workers could not stop for lunch. They had to eat as they worked. The workers already called the new man "Bruiser." Now Bruiser picked up his lunch and went out. "The boss raved and cussed," the woman explained, "almost tearing his hair out because Bruiser had caused the work to slow down. In exactly one hour Bruiser was back."

The boss promptly fired Bruiser. That night after work, the woman laundry worker saw Bruiser again. He said he was a union organizer. Would she come to a meeting?

"As disgusted as I was with my lot, I don't have to tell you that I was the first one to reach the meeting." Almost everyone came. Almost everyone joined the union.

The boss tried to scare the workers. Then he offered to start a different union. He fired some of the old workers. The rest went out on strike. The boss hired **scabs**. Scabs are workers who take the place of strikers.

"They messed up so that the boss called us back to work at union hours, union wages, and better conditions."

Who Speaks for America?

Most people voted for FDR. They thought he was better than other candidates. But they did not agree with everything he said or did.

People had strong opinions. They disagreed on many things. The voice of America was many voices arguing.

CHAPTER 8

Coming Out of the Depression

A New Attitude

In May 1933, the bonus marchers returned to Washington, D. C. These military veterans wanted their bonuses early. They had marched on Washington during President Hoover's term. Hoover used force to turn them away. The marchers thought maybe FDR would listen.

FDR knew he could not give them their bonuses. The money was not there. They would have to wait until 1945. He had sympathy for the marchers. He could not give them what they wanted. But he still wanted to show respect.

FDR ordered that the marchers be met with kindness. They were given shelter at Fort Hunt. They were given coffee and three meals a day. The navy band played for them.

Because of polio, FDR was in a wheelchair. That made travel difficult. Once again, Mrs. Roosevelt became his eyes and ears.

One day, Mrs. Roosevelt came to visit the bonus marchers. She walked through ankle-deep mud. She led the men in song. She listened to their stories. One marcher said that Hoover sent the army, but FDR sent his wife. That was a key difference.

FDR also got jobs for the veterans. He created new CCC jobs. Most of the bonus marchers were given CCC jobs.

Eleanor Roosevelt serving soup to the poor

The Roosevelts cared about the poor. They wanted to help. FDR spoke to people in his Fireside Chats. He let them know that he cared.

Eleanor visited poor people across the country. She climbed down into coal mines. She visited the poor in their homes. She sat down to lunch with African Americans.

A newspaper criticized her visit to a coal mine. She said in reply, "Every woman in public life needs to develop skin as tough as rhinoceros hide." And she kept going.

FDR and Mrs. Roosevelt changed the image of government. They made it their job to care. Each of them had been born into a rich family. Now they belonged to the common people. And so did the government of the United States.

A New Role

The role of government changed in the 1930s. No longer was government **remote** or distant from ordinary people. Now it was involved in daily life. Government made jobs for people. Government regulated businesses. Government fed people. Government built houses. Government gave pensions.

Many people did not like the new role. They thought government was too big. They thought people should be more independent. They did not like government rules.

The New Deal brought a new government. There was no turning back.

The economy responded slowly. Most new jobs were government jobs. Private business took a long time to recover.

In 1938, FDR tried to cut government spending. He thought business could now provide enough jobs. But unemployment rose again. Stock prices fell.

FDR responded quickly. He asked Congress for more money for jobs. Congress did not agree. Congress and the president clashed. Would the nation head back into a depression?

And Then Came War

In Europe, war marched on. Hitler had taken over Germany in the 1930s. In 1939, he took over Czechoslovakia. Then he led the invasion of Poland. England and France declared war on Germany.

"I hope the United States will keep out of this war," FDR said. In a Fireside Chat, he pledged peace "as long as it remains within my power."

Wars kill people, but they sometimes feed economies. That happened during World War I in the United States. Now it was happening again.

Congress agreed to spend half a billion dollars on defense. U.S. industries geared up to produce more. The country prepared for a war it hoped would never come. That preparation created more jobs.

On December 7, 1941, the Japanese bombed Pearl Harbor. The United States entered World War II. The depression era had ended. A new and bloody era was at hand.

USS *Shaw* exploding during Japanese raid on Pearl Harbor

Sources

Books

Cashman, Sean Dennis. *America Ascendant: From Theodore Roosevelt to FDR in the Century of American Power, 1901–1945,* New York University Press, New York, NY, 1998.

McElvaine, Robert S. *The Great Depression: America, 1929-1941,* Random House, New York, NY, 1984, 1993.

Terkel, Studs. *Hard Times: An Oral History of the Great Depression*, The New Press, New York, NY, 1970, 1986.

Tice, D. J. *Dust Bowl Sister*, St. Paul Pioneer Press, St. Paul, MN, 1997.

Watkins, T. H. *The Hungry Years: A Narrative History of the Great Depression in America*, Henry Holt, New York, NY, 1999.

Web Sites

www.geocities.com/oralbio/covingtonbio.html
Biography of Elias W. Covington

www.louisville.edu/~kprayb01/1920s-timeline-page.html
Timeline of the 1920s

www.pbs.org/wgbh/amex/dustbowl/filmmore
Surviving the Dust Bowl

www.lcweb2.loc.gov/ammem/wpaintro/wpahome.html
American Life Histories: Manuscripts from the Federal Writers' Project, 1936-1940
These life histories were written by the staff of the Folklore Project of the Federal Writers' Project for the U.S. Works Progress (later Work Projects) Administration (WPA) from

1936-1940. The Library of Congress collection includes 2,900 documents representing the work of over 300 writers from 24 states. Typically 2,000-15,000 words in length, the documents consist of drafts and revisions, varying in form from narrative to dialogue to report to case history. The histories describe the informant's family, education, income, occupation, political views, religion and mores, medical needs, diet, and miscellaneous observations. Pseudonyms are often substituted for individuals and places named in the narrative texts. Specific histories quoted in this Web site include

Myron Buxton

Raymond Tarver

Elmer Thomas

"Negro Laundry Workers"

"Domestic Workers Union"

Other histories consulted during research include

Arthur R. Goodlett

"Amateur Night in Harlem"

Alfred O. Philipp

Oscar Staub

Charles Seabrook

Arthur W. Bailey

F.W. Johnston

Walter Coachman

Mamie Brown

Mrs. Janie Bradberry Harris

Lilly Lindo

Minnie Stonestreet

James Jackson Butler

Glossary

alien   foreign-born citizen

amendment   change to the United States Constitution that must be approved by a vote of the people

assassinate   to kill

barter   to trade or exchange goods and services

bonus   government payment to those who served during wartime

bootleg   having to do with illegal alcoholic beverages

broker   agent who buys and sells for another person

call in   to order the immediate payment of a loan in full

charity   aid given to those in need

Communist   believing in a government that owns all business and industry

conservative   believing in a political policy based on tradition and social stability

corrupt   relating to the act of using improper or unlawful means, such as bribery

credit   act of making payments for something instead of paying entire amount at the time of purchase

dependent child   minor who depends on an adult for food, shelter, and clothing

depositor   person who puts money in a bank

depression   period of low economic activity marked by rising levels of unemployment

dictator	one who has absolute power
dignity	state of being worthy, honored, or highly thought of
domestic	relating to household duties and chores
erosion	act of being worn away by wind or water
evict	to force out legally
fail	to close due to having more money going out than coming in
immigrant	one who comes from another country or region
in default	unable to pay back a loan
inheritance	relating to property or money received after the death of someone
interest	charge or fee for borrowing money that is usually a percentage of the amount borrowed
market	commercial activity; buying and selling of goods
migrant	having ability to move from one place to another
moratorium	act of stopping an activity
mortgage	loan on property that requires regular payments with interest
patriotism	act of honoring one's country
pension	fixed sum of money paid to a person
Progressive	believing in government of moderate political action and social change
prohibition	act of forbidding the manufacture, transport, or sale of alcoholic beverages

prosperity	condition of being successful with enough money and goods
racism	belief that one race is superior to all others
radical	believing in extreme measures to keep or restore something
raise a gang	term used when new men are being hired
receiver	person appointed to manage and settle debts of a failed (see glossary entry) business
refuge	place that provides shelter or protection
regulate	to place under the control of the government in order to bring order or uniformity to something
relief	aid in the form of money or goods for the needy
remote	faraway
scab	worker who accepts employment or replaces a union worker during a strike
scheme	plan to make money
scrimp	to spend only what is necessary in order to save as much money as possible
security	something given to make certain a loan is repaid
segregation	act of separating
share	certificate showing one of the equal divisions of the capital of a corporation
sharecropper	farmer who is provided with credit for seed, tools, living quarters, and food. The farmer works the land and receives an agreed share of the value of the crop minus charges.

slum	densely populated, urban area having crowded, dirty, run-down housing
Socialist	relating to one who believes that the production and distribution of goods should be controlled by the government. The distribution of goods and pay depends on work done.
sound	solid; stable
spiritual	deeply emotional religious song that was developed by African Americans in the South
stock	value of a corporation that is usually divided into shares
strike	to stop work in order to force employers to agree to employees' demands
tenant	one who rents property
union	organization that represents workers in disputes with management
veteran	person who has served in one of the armed forces
vice	moral failing or corruption
voluntary	acting of one's own free will

Index